Our Changing World

THE TIMELINE LIBRARY

THE HISTORY OF SPACE TRAVEL

BY BARBARA A. SOMERVILL

1700 1800 1900 2000 2100

Content Adviser: Frank H. Winter, Curator, Smithsonian Institution, Washington, D.C.

THE CHILD'S WORLD® • CHANHASSEN, MINNESOTA

The Child's World

Published in the United States of America by The Child's World®
PO Box 326 • Chanhassen, MN 55317-0326 • 800-599-READ • www.childsworld.com

ACKNOWLEDGMENTS
The Child's World®: Mary Berendes, Publishing Director

Editorial Directions, Inc.: E. Russell Primm, Editorial Director; Katie Marsico, Associate Editor and Line Editor; Judith Shiffer, Assistant Editor; Matt Messbarger, Editorial Assistant; Susan Hindman, Copy Editor; Sarah E. De Capua, Proofreader; Peter Garnham, Olivia Nellums, Molly Symmonds, and Stephen Carl Wender, Fact Checkers; Tim Griffin/IndexServ, Indexer; Cian Loughlin O'Day, Photo Researcher; Linda S. Koutris, Photo Selector

The Design Lab: Kathleen Petelinsek, Design and Art Production

PHOTOS
Cover/frontispiece images: NASA (main); NASA/USGS (left inset); NASA/JPL (right inset).

Interior: Bettmann/Corbis: 7, 10, 13, 18; Corbis: 23 (NASA), 27 (Roger Ressmeyer); Getty Images/Hulton|Archive: 9; NASA: 5 (USGS), 15 (Peter Gorin), 16 (KSC), 20 (JSC); NASA/JPL: 25 (Hubble Heritage Team/STScI/AURA), 29.

Timeline: Corbis: 8 (Gianni Dagli Orti), 10 (Stefan Bianchetti), 11 (Bettmann), 17, 25 (Peter Turnley), 26 (Ethan Miller); Getty Images/Warner Bros.: 28; Library of Congress: 6; NASA: 13, 14 (Asif A. Siddiqi), 19, 21 (JSC), 23 (KSC), 24 (Glenn Research Center).

REGISTRATION

LIBRARY OF CONGRESS CATALOGING-IN-PUBLICATION DATA
Somervill, Barbara A.
  The history of space travel / by Barbara A. Somervill.
    p. cm. — (The timeline library (series))
  Includes index.
  ISBN 1-59296-345-5 (library bound : alk. paper) 1. Astronautics—History—Juvenile literature. 2. Manned space flight—Juvenile literature. 3. Interplanetary voyages—Juvenile literature. I. Title. II. Series.
  TL793.S622 2004
  629.45'009—dc22   2004003949

TABLE OF CONTENTS

THE STARS ABOVE

Hassan guides the **probe** close to Europa, one of Jupiter's 61 moons. He must not go too close. Jupiter's moons have gravity, and the probe might be drawn into the moon.

The probe sends back pictures of a network of lines. Hassan decides that the lines are cracks in Europa's ice covering. But what's that in the corner? Hassan clicks his mouse to increase the picture's size. Is it . . . water? Could there be liquid water on Europa? He'll contact Houston about his discovery.

Amila stands in the doorway to Hassan's room. "Earth to Hassan . . . Earth to Hassan," she calls, laughing. "Dinner's on the table, and you're late . . . again."

Hassan closes out his space travel computer program. The monitor returns to the screen saver—the Starship *Enterprise* traveling through galaxies far, far away. What would it be like to travel among the stars? Hassan can only dream.

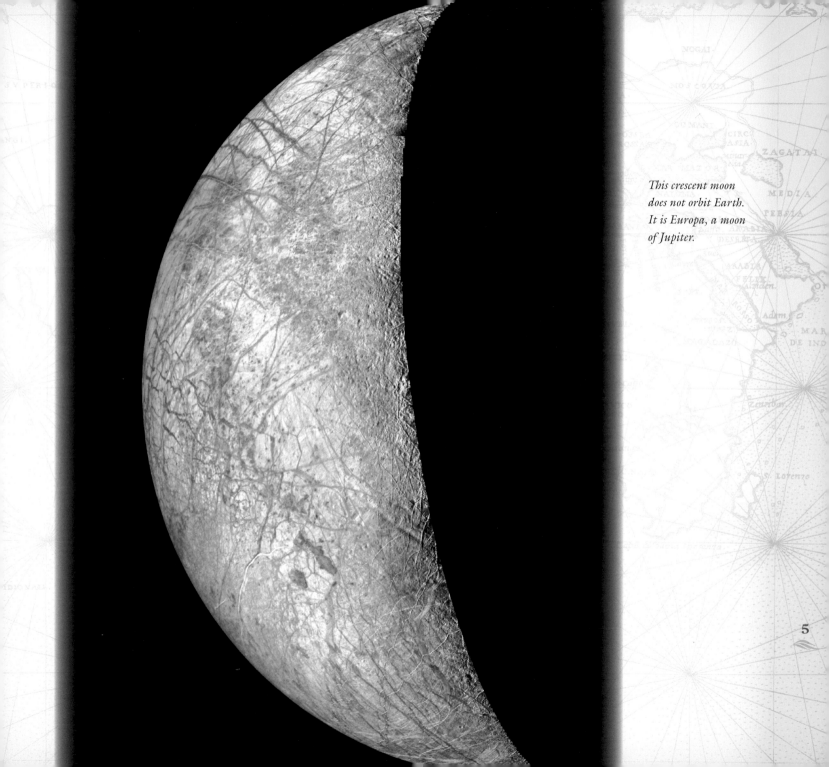

This crescent moon
does not orbit Earth.
It is Europa, a moon
of Jupiter.

CHAPTER ONE
STARGAZERS AND BIG DREAMERS

Thousands of years ago, early humans stared at the night sky in wonder. They saw stars shooting through the dark. In the same way that you might connect the dots, they traced star-to-star pictures—a lion, a bear, a crab. They watched the Moon cross the sky and marked the passing seasons.

Ancient cultures believed that their gods lived among the stars. They thought movement in the skies affected the lives of people on Earth.

Some people drew charts or maps to record those movements. As early as 1500 B.C., the Chinese kept accurate records on star maps. The Babylonians (from what is now Iraq), the Egyptians, and the Mayans of Central America used the stars and Moon to make calendars.

ca. 3000 B.C.

People build stone circles, such as Stonehenge (right) to observe the stars and planets.

Beeswax candles are used in Egypt.

1500 B.C.

The Chinese begin mapping star movements.

The Egyptians improve glassmaking.

300 B.C.–A.D. 165: THE GREEKS

The Greeks were the first people to apply mathematics to stargazing. Early Greek **astronomers** determined that planets and the Sun moved in circles. Aristarchus (ca. 310–230 B.C.) used geometry to figure out the size and distance of the Sun and Moon. His results were way off, but his method for figuring out the answers was correct.

Aristarchus decided that the Sun was the center of the universe. People thought his ideas were very strange. About 100 years later, another Greek, Hipparchus (ca. 190–120 B.C.), claimed the universe revolved around Earth. He also recorded the position and movement of nearly 850 stars. Hipparchus developed a better way to measure the Sun and Moon.

> STONEHENGE
>
> ABOUT 5,000 YEARS AGO, SOME CULTURES BEGAN BUILDING STONE CIRCLES IN OPEN FIELDS. THESE CIRCLES, SUCH AS STONEHENGE IN ENGLAND, MIGHT HAVE BEEN USED TO TRACK THE MOVEMENT OF STARS AND PLANETS. PEOPLE MIGHT HAVE CHECKED THE CHANGING LOCATIONS OF THE SUN AND MOON BY THEIR PLACE AGAINST THE STONES.

200s B.C.		100s B.C.	
Aristarchus claims the Sun is the center of the universe.		Hipparchus suggests that Earth is the center of the universe.	
People begin putting iron shoes on horses.		The Anasazi culture flourishes in what is now southwestern North America.	

Ptolemy (ca. A.D. 100–165), a Roman, collected the ideas of early Greek astronomers. He worked as a librarian at the great library in Alexandria, Egypt. Based on his readings, Ptolemy defined the orbit of the Moon, predicted **lunar eclipses,** and mapped more than 1,000 stars. He grouped these stars into 48 **constellations**—the same constellations we observe today.

A.D. 1500–1600: COPERNICUS, KEPLER, AND GALILEO

Before 1492, when Christopher Columbus arrived in the Americas, most people believed

A.D. 100s

Ptolemy (right) records the positions of more than 1,000 stars.

The Chinese invent paper.

The Greek astronomer Hipparchus studied the stars in Alexandria, Egypt.

the Sun circled the Earth. They also thought Earth was flat. People claimed Columbus's ships would fall off Earth's edge and into . . . well, no one quite knew what.

Then, three scientists turned their eyes to the stars. They were Nicolaus Copernicus, Johannes Kepler, and Galileo Galilei. Over the course of 100 years, these three men changed the way people looked at the universe.

In 1514, Copernicus determined that Earth circled the Sun—not the other way around. His ideas were not made public

Copernicus believed that the Earth traveled around the Sun.

Nicolaus Copernicus determines that the Sun at the center of the universe.

Spanish conquistadors conquer Cuba.

1514

until the year he died, 1543. Copernicus added that Earth spun around as it orbited the Sun. Copernicus said the universe was enormous. His thoughts made human beings seem small and unimportant. The Roman Catholic Church did not accept Copernicus's ideas—so no one else dared to, either.

That is, until 1596, when German astronomer Johannes Kepler wrote that he agreed with Copernicus. Kepler studied the movements of Mars in the night sky. By tracking Mars's path, Kepler proved that planet orbits were not circular, but ellipses or ovals. In a book published four years after his death in 1630, Kepler suggested the possibilities of a trip to the Moon.

1596

Johannes Kepler writes that he agrees with the theories of Copernicus.

English explorer Sir Francis Drake dies.

As a young man in Italy, Galileo Galilei heard about an invention called a telescope that allowed a person to see long distances. He developed an improved version of this invention. Galileo was the first person to study the night sky through a telescope. He said, "I have observed four planets [actually, moons] which have their orbits around Jupiter. . . . I give infinite thanks that I alone have been the first observer of amazing things."

The telescope brought planets into common view. People dreamed of traveling among the stars. However, it would be several more centuries before traveling to the Moon, planets, or stars became a reality.

Galileo Galilei invented a telescope for viewing stars and planets. He named several of Jupiter's moons.

A book by Kepler (right) suggesting the possibility of travel to the Moon is published.

1634

The colony of Maryland is founded.

CHAPTER TWO

EARLY ADVENTURES IN SPACE

Dreaming of space travel and making the dream a reality are two different things. When the Wright brothers took their first flight in 1903, to all but few space travel seemed impossible. After all, airplanes barely flew higher than the trees. The stars were much too far away. Scientific advances were needed before space travel could become more than just a dream.

For centuries, the Chinese filled rockets with gunpowder. Some were fireworks and others were shot toward enemy armies. Scientists realized that the shape of a rocket—a cylinder with a cone on top—would work for space travel. They just had to figure out how to overcome a few problems: developing rockets with sufficient **thrust** to overcome gravity, keeping astronauts alive, and returning to Earth.

1903

Orville and Wilbur Wright
complete their first airplane flight.

Teddy Bears, named for President
Teddy Roosevelt, go on sale.

Gravity is the invisible force that holds items to Earth. All large bodies in the universe have some amount of gravity. To overpower Earth's gravity, a rocket needs to reach speeds of about 25,000 miles (40,000 kilometers) per hour. This is called escape velocity. Solid fuel rockets, such as the early Chinese firework rockets, would never make it.

1926: GODDARD'S ROCKET

For many years, scientist Robert Goddard believed he could make a rocket powered by liquid fuel. In 1926, Goddard tested his liquid-fuel rocket at his Aunt Effie's farm near Worcester, Massachusetts. Four horses pulled a wagon into the field carrying *Nell,* a 10-foot (3-meter)-long rocket ready for liftoff. Goddard used a mix of liquid oxygen and

Goddard's first rocket landed in a cabbage patch.

Robert Goddard (right) proves that liquid fuel can propel a rocket.

1926

A. A. Milne publishes *Winnie the Pooh.*

THE FIRST ROCKET FLIGHT

"THE FIRST FLIGHT WITH A ROCKET USING LIQUID PROPELLANTS WAS MADE YESTERDAY AT AUNT EFFIE'S FARM IN AUBURN. . . . THE ROCKET DID NOT RISE AT FIRST, BUT THE FLAME CAME OUT, AND THERE WAS A STEADY ROAR. AFTER A NUMBER OF SECONDS IT ROSE, SLOWLY UNTIL IT CLEARED THE FRAME. . . . IT LOOKED ALMOST MAGICAL AS IT ROSE."

ROBERT H. GODDARD, 1926

gasoline as fuel. A blowtorch lit the fuel, and within seconds the rocket headed for the sky. *Nell* traveled little more than 40 feet (12 m) before landing in Effie's cabbage patch. Still, this first liquid-fuel rocket launch provided a key to solving the space puzzle.

From 1926 on, engineers found ways to make liquid-fuel rockets travel faster, farther, and with better aim. In 1957, the Soviets shocked the world by launching *Sputnik 1*, the first man-made **satellite.**

At that time, the Soviets and the United States were enemies. Many people believed that control of space might make one nation more powerful than the other. With the launch of *Sputnik 2* only a month later, the Soviet Union

1957

The Soviet Union launches *Sputnik I* (right).

Scientists from 70 countries study the Earth and its cosmic environment during the International Geophysical Year.

1958

The United States launches its first successful satellite, *Explorer I.*

Europe has 160 computers in use; the United States has about 1,000.

declared its goal of winning the space war.

The United States immediately reacted. On December 6, 1957, the United States launched its first *Vanguard* rocket. It performed worse than Goddard's *Nell*. The first *Vanguard* rose only 4 feet (1.2 m) off the launching pad. U.S. space engineers started over. By January 1958, *Explorer 1* took off and placed the first U.S.-made satellite into orbit around the Earth.

1961: A MAN IN SPACE

For several years, satellites left Earth almost as fast as NASA or the Soviet Union could build them. In 1959, the Soviet Union launched their first *Luna* rocket, destined to orbit the Sun. The United States responded with its

NASA

THE NATIONAL AERONAUTICS AND SPACE ADMINISTRATION (NASA) WAS FOUNDED ON OCTOBER 1, 1958. ITS FIRST MISSION WAS *PIONEER 1*, A SPACE PROBE THAT TRAVELED MORE THAN 70,000 MILES (112,000 KM) ABOVE THE EARTH.

Sputnik 2 *carried an interesting passenger: a dog named Laika.*

1959

Tang, a beverage served to astronauts, goes on sale in supermarkets.

U.S.S.R. Premier Nikita Kruschchev visits the United States.

Alan B. Shepard Jr. was the first U.S. astronaut in space.

Moon launches, spy satellites, and weather satellites.

On April 12, 1961, the Soviets launched *Vostok*, a satellite manned by Yuri Gagarin. The spacecraft made one circle around Earth. Three weeks later, NASA launched Mercury capsule *Freedom VII*, which hurled the first U.S. astronaut into space—Alan Shepard.

During the next few years, the United States and the Soviet Union took turns producing space flights. The United States's *Mariner II* passed Venus on its way to orbiting the Sun. In 1965, Soviet Alexei Leonov took the first space walk, lasting 12 minutes. Within three months, NASA astronaut Edward White made a space walk lasting 10 minutes longer than Leonov's. Both nations wanted to dominate space.

1961

Yuri Gagarin becomes the first man in space.

The New York Yankees' Roger Maris hits 61 home runs, breaking Babe Ruth's previous record.

1965

The first space walk lasts 12 minutes.

The Rolling Stones reach No.1 with their hit recording "Satisfaction."

CHAPTER THREE
WALKING ON THE MOON

For eight years, the space race ran on. NASA scientists practiced for their greatest feat: putting a man on the Moon. They had space probes escape Earth's atmosphere and orbit the Moon. They managed a soft lunar landing with another rocket. They built a special vehicle to take astronauts and their spacecraft to the Moon.

Scientists discovered that a lack of gravity—weightlessness (which existed inside the spacecraft)—fooled a body into feeling swollen. They found that drinking plenty of water balanced out the swelling. Astronauts also suffered muscle cramps from being cooped up in a small space. To ease the lack of movement, scientists developed exercises to be scheduled throughout a flight.

Space travel brought new products. Astronauts needed special fireproof

| 1967 | The *Apollo 1* space mission ends in tragedy with three astronauts dying in a launch pad fire. |

The United States is involved in a war in Vietnam.

The U.S. population reaches 200 million.

spacesuits and shaped chairs to protect them during takeoff. Spacesuits had to maintain comfortable body temperatures and ward off harmful rays from the Sun. Astronauts also needed special support sneakers for their feet and sunglasses to protect their eyes.

And, of course, astronauts needed to eat and use a toilet. New freeze-dried foods became space meals. The astronauts even ate freeze-dried ice cream that they squeezed into their mouths through a tube. Using a toilet on Earth depends on gravity. But in space, gravity does not exist. A special space toilet that used suction, like a vacuum cleaner, solved that problem.

1968

2001: A Space Odyssey is released in theatres.

Food-in-a-baggie provided astronauts with meals while in space.

1969: *APOLLO 11*

Apollo 11 became the mission that changed the world. Astronauts Neil Armstrong, Edwin Aldrin, and Michael Collins prepared several years for their Moon flight.

The giant *Saturn V* rocket lifted off from the Kennedy Space Center in Cape Canaveral, Florida on July 16, 1969. The astronauts first orbited around Earth. After one and a half orbits, the *Apollo* spacecraft fired its thrusters and headed toward the Moon. The trip would take four days.

On July 20, 1969, *Apollo 11* reached the Moon. Armstrong and Aldrin entered the lunar **module** *Eagle*. Collins remained on the main spacecraft. At 4:18 eastern standard time, *Eagle* set down on the Moon. On Earth,

1969

Neil Armstrong (right) becomes the first person to set foot on the Moon.

The New York Mets win the World Series.

The Apollo 11 *astronauts had little time to set up scientific experiments. They were only on the Moon for a few hours.*

FOOTPRINTS
ON THE MOON
DUE TO THE LACK OF WIND ON
THE MOON, SCIENTISTS BELIEVE
THAT ARMSTRONG'S AND
ALDRIN'S FOOTPRINTS THERE
WILL PROBABLY REMAIN FOR
MILLIONS OF YEARS. BECAUSE
THERE'S NO ATMOSPHERE,
THERE'S NO WIND TO BLOW THE
DUST AWAY.

NASA heard this message: "Houston, Tranquility Base here. The *Eagle* has landed." The roar of success echoed throughout NASA's home base.

Hours later, Armstrong set foot on the Moon. Aldrin followed shortly after him. Stepping off the lunar module, Armstrong said, "That's one small step for man, one giant leap for mankind."

The astronauts stayed on the Moon's surface for two and a half hours. They planted an American flag that is still there. They also collected rocks to bring back to Earth for study.

The astronauts returned to the *Eagle* and left the Moon. The module docked with the waiting *Apollo* spacecraft. Then the astronauts left lunar orbit and headed home. On July 24,

1969

Neil Armstrong and Edwin Aldrin leave footprints on the moon.

The United States is involved in a war in Vietnam.

1969, the spacecraft splashed down in the Pacific Ocean.

Following such remarkable success, NASA under-took several more *Apollo* missions. Perhaps the most memorable was *Apollo 13*. James Lovell, John Swigert, and Fred Haise took off aboard *Apollo 13* on April 11, 1970.

An explosion damaged the spacecraft's oxygen tanks. Engineers feared they might not be able to bring *Apollo 13* home.

Scientists worked nonstop to find solutions to the spacecraft's problems. They told the astronauts how to repair their spaceship. Finally, *Apollo 13* left lunar orbit and headed for Earth. When *Apollo 13* splashed down, people around the world breathed a sigh of relief.

> "CONTROL OF SPACE MEANS CONTROL OF THE WORLD. . . . THAT IS THE ULTIMATE POSITION: THE POSITION OF TOTAL CONTROL OVER THE EARTH THAT LIES SOMEWHERE IN OUTER SPACE."
> LYNDON B. JOHNSON, U.S. PRESIDENT

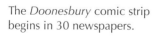

1970

Apollo 13 (right) overcomes technical problems and returns safely to Earth.

The *Doonesbury* comic strip begins in 30 newspapers.

William Armstrong's *Sounder* wins the Newbery Medal for best children's book.

CHAPTER FOUR
SPACE SHUTTLES AND TERRIFIC TELESCOPES

S pace flights were not all about the Moon. Unmanned trips to Venus, Mars, and beyond became frequent. Women joined space crews. Scientists built space laboratories, manned by Soviet **cosmonauts** or American astronauts. NASA developed shuttles that flew into space, returned, and were used again.

Manned space stations went into orbit as early as 1971. The Soviet Union's *Salyut 1* became the first laboratory in space. The station weighed 40,700 pounds (18,460 kilograms) and was a 46-foot (14-m)-long cylinder. The Soviet Union had planned to send cosmonauts to work on *Salyut 1*. But the first attempt to connect with the space station failed. The crew could not get the hatch to open.

1971

The Soviets launch the first space station.

The United States lowers the voting age from 21 to 18.

The next attempt, *Soyuz 11*, proved more successful. They were able to get the *Salyut I* hatch to open and entered the station. This became the first manned use of a space laboratory. Unfortunately, the *Soyuz II* developed hatch problems. The cosmonauts died on their return trip.

The United States launched its first space laboratory, *Skylab*, in 1973. Three crews manned *Skylab* and kept it working. *Skylab* and *Salyut 1* taught scientists about the effects of staying in space for a long time. Crews took pictures of Earth and stars and ran experiments. An onboard greenhouse provided information about growing plants in space.

1981: THE SPACE SHUTTLE

NASA realized that a regular, reusable vehicle for trips to

Three crews of astronauts kept Skylab *in good working order.*

The first space shuttle (right) takes flight.

MTV begins broadcasting.

Prince Charles and Lady Diana are married in London, England.

Skylab was needed. They launched the first manned mission of the space shuttle *Columbia* on April 12, 1981. Four shuttles—*Columbia, Discovery, Atlantis,* and *Challenger*—have made about 100 trips in space. The shuttles have carried satellites and placed them in orbit. They allowed astronauts to visit, supply, and repair space stations. Shuttle astronauts performed scientific experiments, including testing **zero gravity** using a Slinky.

A space shuttle launch is an exciting event. The shuttle is mounted on the side of a rocket. As the rocket speeds upward, the shuttle is hurled into space. Although shuttles have engines, they fly and land more like gliders.

Even with 100 shuttle successes, people most often

1983

Sally Ride (right) becomes the first U.S. woman in space.

Harold Washington becomes the first African-American mayor of Chicago.

1986

The space shuttle *Challenger* explodes shortly after takeoff.

Sarah, Plain and Tall wins the Newbery Medal.

remember NASA's failures. In 1986, the shuttle *Challenger* exploded shortly after takeoff. Its crew was killed. In 2003, the *Columbia* burned up on reentry.

1990: THE HUBBLE TELESCOPE

One of the space shuttle's largest payloads was the Hubble Space Telescope. Put in orbit in 1990, the Hubble telescope has provided scientists with a fascinating and very far reaching view of outer space.

Hubble's advantage is its position above Earth's atmosphere. It has a clear view of the stars, galaxies, planets, and meteors. Hubble has revealed more than 1,500 galaxies. A new, more powerful telescope may one day replace the Hubble telescope in the early 2000s.

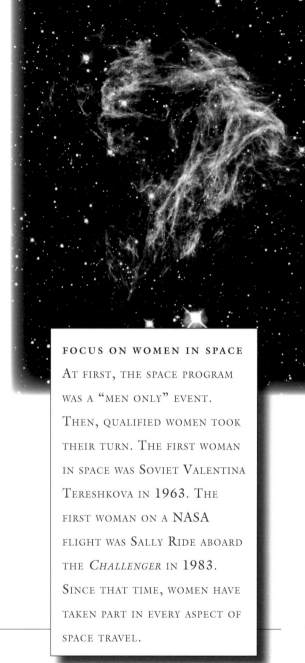

FOCUS ON WOMEN IN SPACE
AT FIRST, THE SPACE PROGRAM WAS A "MEN ONLY" EVENT. THEN, QUALIFIED WOMEN TOOK THEIR TURN. THE FIRST WOMAN IN SPACE WAS SOVIET VALENTINA TERESHKOVA IN 1963. THE FIRST WOMAN ON A NASA FLIGHT WAS SALLY RIDE ABOARD THE *CHALLENGER* IN 1983. SINCE THAT TIME, WOMEN HAVE TAKEN PART IN EVERY ASPECT OF SPACE TRAVEL.

The Hubble telescope begins sending pictures of faraway stars back to Earth.

1990

The first McDonald's in the Soviet Union (left) opens in Moscow.

The Hubble telescope took this picture of the universe's greatest fireworks: a stellar explosion.

CHAPTER FIVE

THE MOON AGAIN . . . THEN MARS

Today, space is not limited to Russia and the United States. In 1998, Japan launched its *Nozomi* probe to Mars. The Chinese sent up the *Shenzhou* in 2001, carrying a monkey, a dog, and a rabbit. Astronauts have been Ukrainian, Japanese, and Israeli. Space has become an international playground.

The Russians launched a massive space station called *Mir* in 1986. Up to six different spacecraft could dock at *Mir*. This station hosted astronauts from Russia, the United States, and Australia.

The new International Space Station (ISS) has taken over for *Mir*. This is a joint project among 16 nations, including Canada, Brazil, Russia, Japan, the United States, and the 11 members of the European Space Agency. The ISS is

1998

The Japanese launch the *Nozomi* Mars probe.

Celine Dion (right) sings "My Heart Will Go On," the year's top song.

made of modules that join together like pieces of a puzzle. The Russians launched the first part of the new station—*Zarya*—in November 1998. The space shuttle *Endeavour* carried the second part—*Unity*—into space a month later. When finished, the ISS will be about the size of two football fields.

2000: SPACE PROBES

The year 2000 began with *Galileo,* a space probe, reaching Jupiter's ice moon, Europa. The meeting of the two was special because, in 1610, Galileo Galilei was the first human to see Europa.

The central living unit of the ISS—*Zvezda*—linked with *Zarya* and *Unity* in July 2000. Other missions to the space station carried robotic arms, antennae, and laboratory

Scientists tested the Galileo *probe thoroughly before launching.*

Galileo reaches the ice moon Europa.
Expedition One crew arrives on the International Space Station.

2000

The summer Olympics are held in Sydney, Australia.

SLEEPING ON *MIR*
WHEN THE CREW ON *MIR* SLEPT, THEY CURLED UP IN BAGS TIED TO THE WALL. WITHOUT THE BAGS, SLEEPING SPACE TRAVELERS MIGHT HAVE FLOATED AROUND IN THE ZERO GRAVITY STATION.

units. NASA's *Discovery* arrived at the ISS in March 2001 with the *Leonardo* module, built by Italy. That same month, *Mir* left orbit, broke up in Earth's atmosphere, and crashed into the Pacific Ocean.

2004: ROAMING ON MARS

The big news in space came with the launches of NASA's Mars rovers in 2003. *Spirit* lifted off on June 10, with *Opportunity* following on July 7. The trips to Mars each took about six months.

Rovers are exploration vehicles. One of their goals was to analyze soil and rocks on Mars. The rovers took fresh rock samples and determined what elements made up the rocks. The rovers may be the first step in a "man-on-

2001

The Chinese launch *Shenzhou* with a monkey, a dog, and a rabbit on board.

Harry Potter and the Sorcerer's Stone (right) is the number one moneymaking movie.

Mars" program. Knowing what elements exist on the planet will help scientists prepare for such a mission.

Scientists plan years in advance for trips into space. In 2004, President George W. Bush said he hoped to see NASA build a human settlement on the Moon. In addition, he wanted NASA to plan a manned mission to Mars.

Today's 10-year-old children may live to see regular shuttles between the Earth and the Moon. People may found colonies on Mars . . . or on distant planets. They may even take "winter" vacations on the ice moons of Jupiter. But that is the stuff of dreamers and stargazers.

2004

Spirit and *Opportunity* send back pictures from Mars.

The United States continues military actions in Afghanistan and Iraq.

This is Mars as seen by the Spirit *rover.*

astronomers (uh-STRON-uh-murz) Astronomers are scientists who study the solar system and outer space. Early Greek astronomers determined that planets and the Sun moved in circles.

constellations (kon-stuh-LAY-shuhnz) Constellations are groups of stars that form shapes or patterns. Ptolemy grouped stars into 48 constellations.

cosmonauts (KOZ-mo-nawts) Cosmonauts are Russian astronauts. Cosmonaut Yuri Gagarin was the first man in space.

lunar eclipses (LOO-nur i-KLIPS-ez) In a lunar eclipse, the Earth comes between the Moon and the Sun so that all or part of the Moon's light is blocked from viewing on Earth. Ptolemy predicted lunar eclipses.

module (MOJ-ool) A module is a part or unit. The International Space Station is made of modules that join together like pieces of a puzzle.

probe (PROHB) A probe is a tool or device used for exploration. *Galileo,* a space probe, reached Jupiter's ice moon, Europa, in 2000.

satellite (SAT-uh-lite) A satellite is a man-made moon. The Russians launched their first satellite in 1957.

thrust (THRUHST) Thrust is the power or force that propels a device forward. Goddard's rocket had too little thrust to travel very far.

zero gravity (ZIHR-oh GRAV-uh-tee) Zero gravity is a state of weightlessness in space. The astronauts aboard the space station learned to work in zero gravity.

AT THE LIBRARY

Nonfiction

Gribbin, Mary, and John R. Gribbin. *Eyewitness Science: Time and Space.* New York: DK Publishing, 2000.

* Hopping, Lorraine Jean. *Sally Ride: Space Pioneer.* New York: McGraw-Hill, 2000.

Nardo, Don. *Space Travel.* San Diego: Kidhaven, 2003.

* Scheller, William. *Spaced Out!: An Extreme Reader, from Warps and Wormholes to Killer Asteroids.* New York: Planet Dexter, 1999.

Stott, Carole. *Backpack Books: 1001 Facts about Space.* New York: DK Publishing, 2002.

Wunsch, Susi Trautmann. *The Adventures of Sojourner: The Mission to Mars That Thrilled the World.* Buffalo, N.Y.: Firefly Press, 1998.

Fiction

Morrissey, Dean. *The Moon Robber.* New York: HarperCollins, 2001.

* Books marked with a star are challenge reading material for those reading above grade level.

ON THE WEB

Visit our home page for lots of links about space travel: *http://www.childsworld.com/links.html*

Note to Parents, Teachers, and Librarians:
We routinely check our Web links to make sure they're safe, active sites—so encourage your readers to check them out!

PLACES TO VISIT OR CONTACT

The Air Force Space and Missile Museum
Cape Canaveral Air Force Station
Cape Canaveral, FL 32920
321/452-2121

National Air and Space Museum
6th and Independence Avenue SW
Washington, DC 20560
202/357-2700

U.S. Space Camp
PO Box 070015
Huntsville, AL 35807-7015
800/533-7281

INDEX

32

ABOUT THE AUTHOR

Barbara A. Somervill is the author of many books for children. She loves learning and sees every writing project as a chance to learn new information or gain a new understanding. Ms. Somervill grew up in New York State, but has also lived in Toronto, Canada; Canberra, Australia; California; and South Carolina. She currently lives with her husband in Simpsonville, South Carolina.